MOTIVATING PEOPLE

ROBERT HELLER

DK PUBLISHING, INC.

A DK PUBLISHING BOOK

Editor David Tombesi-Walton
Project Art Editor Ian Midson
US Editor Irene Pavitt
Designer Laura Watson

DTP Designer Jason Little
Production Controllers Silvia La Greca,
Michelle Thomas

Series Editor Jane Simmonds
Series Art Editor Tracy Hambleton-Miles

Managing Editor Stephanie Jackson
Managing Art Editor Nigel Duffield

First American Edition, 1998
6 8 10 9 7 5

Published in the United States by
DK Publishing, Inc.
95 Madison Avenue
New York, New York 10016

Visit us on the World Wide Web at http://www.dk.com

Library of Congress Cataloging-in-Publication Data
Heller, Robert, 1932–
    Motivating People / by Robert Heller
        p.   cm. -- (Essential managers)
    Includes index.
    ISBN 0-7894-2896-2
    1. Employee motivation. I. Title. II. Series.
HF5549.5.M63H45   1998
658.3'14--dc21   98–15313
                                             CIP

Reproduced by Colourscan, Singapore
Printed in Hong Kong by Wing King Tong Co. Ltd.

CONTENTS

GETTING THE BEST FROM PEOPLE

REWARDING ACHIEVEMENT

INTRODUCTION

Today's increasingly competitive business world means that a highly motivated workforce is vital for any organization seeking to achieve good results. Therefore, learning how to motivate others has become an essential skill for managers. Motivating People shows you how best to put motivational theories into practice to create and sustain a positive environment in the workplace. The book contains a wealth of practical advice, including 101 quick-reference tips scattered throughout, while all the important motivational techniques are comprehensively explained – from analyzing the needs of different staff members, to offering incentives and using multiskilling and training to increase job satisfaction. A self-assessment test at the end of the book evaluates your motivational skills, helping you raise performance levels and get the most from both yourself and your staff.

ANALYZING MOTIVATION

To inspire people to work – individually or in groups –
in ways that produce the best results, you need to tap into
their own personal motivational forces.

WHAT IS MOTIVATION?

The art of motivating people starts with learning how to influence individuals' behavior. Once you understand this, you are more likely to achieve the results that both the organization and its members want.

1 If you do not know what motivates a person, just ask.

▲ **BEING MOTIVATED**
For an employee, the chief advantage of being motivated is job satisfaction. For the employer, it means high-quality work.

DEFINING MOTIVATION

Motivation is the will to act. It was once assumed that motivation had to be injected from outside, but it is now understood that everyone is motivated by several differing forces. In the workplace, seek to influence your staff to align their own motivations with the needs of the organization.

To release the full potential of employees, organizations are rapidly moving away from "command and control" and toward "advise and consent" as a way of motivating. This change of attitude began when employers recognized that rewarding good work is more effective than threatening punitive measures for bad work.

MOTIVATING LONG TERM

Self-motivation is long-lasting. Inspire self-motivated staff further by trusting them to work on their own initiatives and encouraging them to take responsibility for entire tasks. For demotivated staff members, find out what would motivate them and implement whatever help you can. Highly motivated individuals are vital to supply organizations with the new initiatives that are necessary in the competitive business world.

2 Assess your own motivation levels as well as those of your staff.

WHOM TO MOTIVATE?

Motivation used to be considered only in one direction: downward, the superior motivating the subordinate. That is no longer enough. In well-managed organizations, in which subordinates do far more than take orders, superiors may need motivating to act accordingly. Encourage colleagues to share your ideas and enthusiasm at work. Use motivation to achieve both collaboration and cooperation from everyone with whom you work.

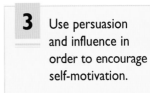

3 Use persuasion and influence in order to encourage self-motivation.

MOTIVATING DIFFERENT PEOPLE IN DIFFERENT WAYS

MANAGER
As a manager, it is important to remember that you should use your motivational techniques to influence not only subordinates, but also your colleagues and managers senior to yourself.

SENIOR MANAGER
Motivate superiors to perceive that what you request suits their own purposes: for instance, improving management information with a new system.

COLLEAGUE
Motivate colleagues to feel that by helping and supporting you they are pursuing their own ends: for example, putting together a joint plan for office economies.

SUBORDINATE
Motivate subordinates to think that following your wishes will bring them satisfaction: for instance, taking over responsibility for an entire job.

RECOGNIZING NEEDS

Since the 1940s, research into human behavior has suggested that people are motivated by a number of different needs, at work and in their personal lives. Recognizing and satisfying these needs will help you to get the best from people.

4 Establish what the needs of your staff are, and assist in meeting them.

UNDERSTANDING MOTIVATION

Several motivation theories work on the assumption that given the chance and the right stimuli, people work well and positively. As a manager, be aware of what these stimuli or "motivational forces" are. Theorist Abraham Maslow grouped them into five areas. The first is physiological needs, and they are followed by further needs, classed as "safety," "social," "esteem," and "self-actualization." According to Maslow, the needs are tackled in order: as you draw near to satisfying one, the priority of the next one becomes higher. Also, once a need has been satisfied, it is no longer a stimulus.

5 Remember that making work fun does not mean making it easy.

SELF-ACTUALIZATION
Realizing individual potential; winning; achieving

ESTEEM NEEDS
Being well regarded by other people; appreciation

SOCIAL NEEDS
Interaction with other people; having friends

SAFETY NEEDS
A sense of security; absence of fear

PHYSIOLOGICAL NEEDS
Warmth; shelter; food; sex – a human being's "animal" needs

▲ THE MASLOW HIERARCHY

Abraham Maslow believed that satisfying just physiological and safety needs is not enough to motivate a person fully. Once these needs have been appeased, there are others waiting to take their place. The Maslow hierarchy can be applied to every aspect of life, and the more ambitious and satisfied the personality, the greater the potential contribution to the organization.

MEETING NEEDS AT WORK

The Maslow hierarchy is particularly relevant in the workplace because individuals need not just money and rewards, but also respect and interaction. When designing jobs, working conditions, and organizational structures, bear in mind the full range of needs in the Maslow hierarchy. Doing this will cost no more, but it will undoubtedly generate higher psychological and economic rewards all around.

6 Try to motivate through the use of *voluntary* social and sports activities.

BALANCING GROUP NEEDS

Individuals acting as part of a group have needs that differ from those of the group. However, it is important for individuals to feel they belong. Find a way to balance the needs of the group with those of individuals. For example, tell staff that if the group meets its major objectives, you may be able to satisfy individual requirements. Do not, of course, promise what you cannot deliver.

7 Use interteam competition to help stimulate team spirit.

MOTIVATION OUTSIDE THE WORKPLACE

One of the areas in which individuals tend to satisfy their motivational needs outside work is sports activities. It is interesting to note the effort that people put into such endeavors, for which they are unlikely to gain material reward. Try to motivate your staff to apply as much effort in the workplace as they would in a team sports event by making work as much fun as possible. A shrewd motivational strategy is to encourage your staff to take up team activities outside the workplace in order to improve their teamwork skills.

▲ **HIRING SPORTS PEOPLE**
Some companies find that staff who are involved in regular sports activities are more likely to enjoy cooperative teamwork in the workplace.

SATISFYING BASIC NEEDS

Psychologist Frederick Herzberg developed a "two-factor" theory for motivation based on "motivators" and "hygiene factors." Hygiene factors – basic human needs at work – do not motivate, but failure to meet them causes dissatisfaction. These factors can be as seemingly trivial as parking space or as vital as sufficient vacation time, but the most important hygiene factor is money. A manager should try to fulfill staff members' financial needs. People require certain pay levels to meet their needs, and slow income progression and ineffective incentives quickly demotivate. Insecurity in a job also greatly demotivates staff.

POINTS TO REMEMBER

- The effects of getting hygiene factors right are only temporary.
- The results of getting hygiene factors wrong can cause long-lasting problems.
- The more choice people can exercise over both hygiene factors and motivators, the better motivated they will be.
- Job insecurity undermines motivation at all levels.
- Recognizing good work is as important as rewarding it.

ESTABLISHING BASIC NEEDS AT WORK

HYGIENE FACTORS	DEFINITIONS
SALARY AND BENEFITS	These include basic income, fringe benefits, bonuses, vacation time, company car, and similar items.
WORKING CONDITIONS	These conditions include working hours, workplace layout, facilities, and equipment provided for the job.
COMPANY POLICY	The company policy is the rules and regulations – formal and informal – that govern employers and employees.
STATUS	A person's status is determined by rank, authority, and relationship to others, reflecting a level of acceptance.
JOB SECURITY	This is the degree of confidence that the employee has regarding continued employment in an organization.
SUPERVISION AND AUTONOMY	This factor concerns the extent of control that an individual has over the content and execution of a job.
OFFICE LIFE	This is the level and type of interpersonal relations within the individual's working environment.
PERSONAL LIFE	An individual's personal life is the time spent on family, friends, and interests – restricted by time spent at work.

ENSURING MOTIVATION

The second of Herzberg's two factors is a set of motivators that actually drive people to achieve. These are what a manager should aim to provide in order to maintain a satisfied workforce. How much a person enjoys achievement depends purely on its recognition. The ability to achieve, in turn, rests on having an enjoyable job and responsibility. The greater that responsibility, the more the individual can feel the satisfaction of advancement. Motivators are built around obtaining growth and "self-actualization" from tasks. You can raise motivation in your staff by increasing their responsibility, thereby "enriching" their jobs.

8 Keep the number of supervisors to a minimum.

9 Remember that different people are motivated in different ways.

HEIGHTENING WORKPLACE MOTIVATION

MOTIVATORS	WHY THEY WORK
ACHIEVEMENT	Reaching or exceeding task objectives is particularly important because the "onward-and-upward" urge to achieve is a basic human drive. It is one of the most powerful motivators and a great source of satisfaction.
RECOGNITION	The acknowledgment of achievements by senior staff members is motivational because it helps enhance self-esteem. For many staff members, recognition may be viewed as a reward in itself.
JOB INTEREST	A job that provides positive, satisfying pleasure to individuals and groups will be a greater motivational force than a job that does not sustain interest. As far as possible, responsibilities should be matched to individuals' interests.
RESPONSIBILITY	The opportunity to exercise authority and power may demand leadership skills, risk-taking, decision-making, and self-direction, all of which raise self-esteem and are strong motivators.
ADVANCEMENT	Promotion, progress, and rising rewards for achievement are important here. Possibly the main motivator, however, is the feeling that advancement is possible. Be honest about promotion prospects and the likely timescale involved.

UNDERSTANDING BEHAVIOR

Actual behavior is very important, but so are the reasons behind it. In most cases, the only way to know how motivated your staff members are is through the ways in which they behave. This includes what they say, their gestures, expressions, and stance.

10 Be aware that the systems that your staff use may be demotivating.

11 Look for positive responses to any criticisms – they are good signs of motivation in staff.

READING BEHAVIOR

When trying to read behavior, recognize that while body language can give clues to motivation levels, it can also be misread. More concrete signals will be provided by the ways in which individuals perform their tasks: this is likely to give you the clearest indication of their motivation. People who work cheerfully and efficiently are unlikely to be hiding anything if they greet you with a smile. Likewise, a dour facial expression should be interpreted adversely only if combined with a grumpy "That's-not-my-job" attitude to work.

SEEING ENTHUSIASM

Positive motivation is often signaled by positive gestures: a smile, an eager pose, and a relaxed manner. When people carry out a task in which they are interested or enthusiastic, they may have a "sparkle" in the eyes, since their pupils actually enlarge. Confident eye contact is also important as a measure of motivation: demotivated people are less likely to look you straight in the eye. Blushing can indicate pleasure, while an increased rate of breathing can indicate enthusiasm – both of these are good signs of motivation.

12 Maintain eye contact with your staff whenever you speak with them.

RECOGNIZING MOTIVATION

Motivation can be recognized in a number of ways – look particularly for signs that your staff feel useful, optimistic, or able to take opportunities. A team in which each member looks after the others' interests is likely to be a good source of motivation. Look for evidence that your staff are satisfied in their jobs rather than anxious or frustrated. If you find no such signs, ask them whether they are satisfied. You can also establish a good idea of an individual's level of motivation by his or her attitude toward work. The statements below are all indicative of motivated staff members:

- They freely volunteer effort and ideas, as well as other contributions;
- They always react well to requests and new assignments;
- They work to achieve, not "to rule";
- They seem to be happy at work;
- They always respond frankly to questions.

13 Ask your staff if any changes at work would help motivate them.

14 Learn to see the difference between work problems and personal ones.

▼ RECOGNIZING A MOTIVATED WORKER

A tidy, organized work space and a well-groomed appearance can indicate a positive attitude to work. A neat desk is a sign of a motivated worker who wishes to be able to find the things they need easily, while attention to personal appearance suggests a high level of commitment to the job.

Cheerful expression is combined with smart appearance

Paperwork is kept neatly

Only task at hand is on desk

Tidy in-box shows that work is up-to-date

REDUCING DEMOTIVATION

Workplace demotivation for many people tends to be caused by poor systems or work overload. Very clear signs of demotivation include high levels of absenteeism and quick turnover of staff. Recognizing demotivation is pointless unless you intend to eradicate its causes. Remember, too, that poor behavior and underperformance are not necessarily signs of workplace demotivation. If demotivation remains even when the situation is improved, it may be due to personal problems.

15 Keep work as varied as possible to avoid causing demotivation.

SEEING NEGATIVE SIGNS

Demotivation may not always be obvious, but look out for defensive, protective actions, such as folding the arms when seated or clenching the fists involuntarily. Inattention, the first sign of demotivation, may be seen in facial expressions, though tapping fingers and restlessness are also negative indicators. A sloppy, "couldn't-care-less" attitude and a lack of enthusiasm for work may also be observed. A monotonous tone of voice may tell of boredom, but be aware also of signs of aggression, such as chopping motions of the hand or pointing a finger in an accusatory manner.

16 Treat departures and absenteeism as warning signs of demotivation.

NOTICING NEGATIVE ▼ APPEARANCE

This person seated at his work station conveys a very negative impression. The disheveled appearance and disorganized desk suggest a careless attitude to work, while the head propped on his hand is a classic sign of boredom.

Hand propping up head may indicate lack of motivation

Untidy pile of papers points to inefficiency

MEASURING MORALE

It is important to measure workplace morale on a regular basis to discover if and why staff are experiencing problems. However, if you notice a rise in departures, suspect that motivation is low, or find that absenteeism is increasing, do not wait to take the workplace "temperature": do it now. You may wish to try using employee attitude surveys; these give a broad indication of morale but can be lengthy and costly. Read the signs from your own talks with people, such as annual appraisals, or set up focus groups or one-to-one interviews. Another way to measure morale is to take a random opinion poll. Remember, however, that if you investigate staff attitudes you must act on the findings, or risk causing further demotivation.

POINTS TO REMEMBER

● Measuring the workplace morale of your staff should be a continual process.

● Lack of motivation may have many causes – do not jump to conclusions about them.

● Inquiring into attitudes carries with it an implicit promise of reform, which must be kept.

● You may not always get honest responses when questioning demotivated staff about their motivation levels.

● Exit interviews with departing staff can give valuable clues as to what is right or wrong with your motivational management.

WAYS OF MEASURING MORALE

METHODS	FACTORS TO CONSIDER
ATTITUDE QUESTIONNAIRES Providing questionnaires to be filled in by all staff members at regular intervals.	● Must be sent to home address to ensure individual attention. ● Follow-up required to obtain satisfactory reply rate. ● Questions need expert drafting, which may be expensive. ● Better for trends rather than showing entire situation.
OPINION POLLS Surveying attitudes on a sample basis (that is, a random selection of the workforce).	● Can be repeated more often than full-scale surveys. ● Lacks the motivational impact of asking everybody. ● Lacks depth, but can be continually revised or refined. ● Good for follow-up on management reforms.
UNSTRUCTURED INTERVIEWS Arranging for employees to meet an outside interviewer one-to-one to talk about the company.	● Can elicit buried concerns and shared difficulties. ● Seems unscientific, but results match questionnaires'. ● Process itself generates improvement in staff morale. ● Interviewer must be careful to avoid overinfluence.
FOCUS GROUPS Arranging for employees to meet an outside interviewer in small groups to discuss company issues.	● Useful insights surface more than in attitude surveys. ● Needs experienced handling by the outside interviewer. ● If too structured, may prevent real concerns from arising. ● Problems tend to be either exaggerated or understated.

BUILDING UP MOTIVATION

Before staff can be receptive to your motivational techniques, you must make sure that the environment in which they work meets a number of important human needs.

ASSESSING YOUR ATTITUDE

It is important that you understand your attitude toward your subordinates. Your thinking will be influenced by your experience and will shape the way in which you behave toward all the people you meet.

17 Be sure staff know their role and its importance.

18 Demonstrate your competence at every opportunity.

19 Improve order and control by using collaborative management.

KNOWING YOUR STYLE

The forces that drive managers will strongly influence motivational behavior. It is important, therefore, to understand your own assumptions and priorities, paying particular attention to your personal and corporate ambitions, so you can motivate others effectively. If you put your job first, you are probably highly motivated and know your career will benefit from success. However, success is not just about meeting task objectives, but also about building an efficient, creative team that will succeed even in your absence. For this, a "share-and-collaborate" style may be more effective than an authoritarian "command-and-control" method.

EVALUATING YOUR TENDENCIES

Theorist Douglas McGregor defined two sets of management styles, which he labeled Theory X and Theory Y. Theory-X managers believe their staff respond mainly to the rewarding carrot and the disciplinary stick. Theory-Y managers, however, believe their staff find work to be a source of satisfaction and will strive to do their best at all times. Most people are not entirely X or Y, but fall somewhere in between. The X and Y theories apply not only to individuals but to organizations as well; indeed, Theory-X managers and habits will often be found in Theory-Y organizations, and vice versa. Study the statements below to judge which of the theories best describes you and your organization.

THEORY X

- If I did not drive my people constantly, they would not get on with their work.
- I sometimes have to fire somebody or tongue-lash them to encourage others.
- Leaders have to lead by making all key decisions themselves.
- I find that most people are unambitious and must be forced to raise their sights.
- I keep my distance from the team since it is necessary for effective command.

THEORY Y

- If somebody falls down on the job, I first ask myself what I did wrong.
- I should sometimes take a back seat at meetings and let others take the lead.
- If I ask someone for their opinion on an issue, I try to do as they suggest.
- People should appraise their bosses as well as be appraised by them.
- Anyone can have creative, innovative ideas if they are encouraged.

▲ MANAGING BY THEORY X
A typical Theory-X manager is likely to keep away from his or her workforce much of the time. In fact, the only time the two meet is when orders or reprimands are to be given.

▲ MANAGING BY THEORY Y
Collaborating with staff over decisions to be made, and getting feedback before implementing decisions, are traits that tend to be typical of a Theory-Y manager. This approach is often more motivating than that of Theory X.

BEING A GOOD MANAGER

Managers often take courses to learn leadership, but good leaders are not necessarily good managers. Leadership is only one part of being a manager, and while a successful manager needs leadership skills, other abilities are equally important.

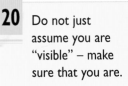

20 Do not just assume you are "visible" – make sure that you are.

21 If bad results occur, review your own motivation as well as employees'.

MANAGING TO MOTIVATE

An essential foundation for motivation is a positive workplace environment created by you, the manager. Employees have the right to expect fair treatment and understanding. They also expect professional competence, part of which includes delegating tasks in order to increase staff members' self-management and participation.

Establish a system that is constructive – not obstructive – in which people can hope to perform at their best. Ascertain where your employees' strengths and interests lie, and then delegate responsibilities that will both exploit these and meet the needs of the organization.

ASSESSING QUALITIES ▼

There are a number of important qualities that a manager must possess in order to motivate staff effectively. If any one of these qualities is absent or deficient, staff will quickly lose their motivation.

Places trust in people

Collaborates with staff

Is loyal to colleagues

Commits to work

Avoids "office politics"

A GOOD MANAGER

POINTS TO REMEMBER

- A poor system accounts for 85 percent of all underperformance.
- People will not perform at their best for uncommitted managers.
- Staff should be treated as friends, allies, partners, and colleagues.
- It is important to have clear directives from your managers to help you to give clear orders.
- The team's objectives are everybody's business, not just the manager's.

TREATING STAFF WELL

When considering how best to treat your staff remember the old adage, "Do unto others as you would be done by." Demonstrate trust in your staff, and prove yourself worthy of trust. This trust includes, on the part of the manager:

- Never making promises that you are not able or are not intending to keep;
- Never asking others to do anything that you would not do yourself;
- Letting your people know that they can count on your respect and your loyalty, unless and until they prove to be undeserving.

To the best of your ability, see to it that working conditions, pay and status issues, job security, and working atmosphere are managed promptly and in a way that is comfortable to employees. Deal with personal problems, which arise from time to time, in a sympathetic and positive manner.

CULTURAL DIFFERENCES

The command-and-control style of management still prevails in the US, despite the more relaxed style found on the West Coast. Japan uniquely combines domination with participation. Collaborative ideas have gained more ground in the UK than in the rest of Europe.

22 Show respect to your staff, and they will show it to you.

CALCULATING YOUR MOTIVATION

Staff will not commit to an uncommitted manager, so it is important that you motivate yourself as well as others. Consider the question, "Am I committed to my objectives and my staff?" The amount of energy you put into your work will indicate your level of motivation. If you are reluctant to begin necessary tasks, unable to make decisions, or prefer office politics to achievement, these are all signs that you are demotivated.

HARNESSING MOTIVATION

Motivation depends on having clear objectives, which will be achieved with good management. Since motivation is personal, aim to align staff's individual drives with the company's purposes in general and your unit's in particular.

In "Management by Objectives" (MBO) systems, objectives are written down for each level of the organization, and individuals are given specific aims and targets. The principle behind this is to ensure that people know what the organization is trying to achieve, what their part of the organization must do to meet those aims, and how, as individuals, they are expected to help. This presupposes that the organization's programs and methods have been fully considered. If they have not, start by constructing team objectives and asking team members to share in the process.

IMPROVING COMMUNICATION

Not communicating at all conveys a very powerful message – the last one that a committed manager wants to deliver. You can never communicate too much, but be careful about the content and delivery of a message so that it inspires motivation.

23 Strengthen your message by using several means of communication.

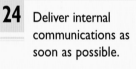

24 Deliver internal communications as soon as possible.

PROVIDING INFORMATION

The ideal approach when providing information is that everybody should know about everything that concerns them directly or indirectly, in full and accurate detail, as soon as possible. Always aim for the ideal: overkill is better than underprovision. Preselect the information that your staff have told you they want – responding to demand is motivational – as well as the information that you want them to know. Once these lists of requirements are established, supply regular updates. Set up a help desk for "other queries," and always inform before rumors arise.

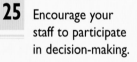

25 Encourage your staff to participate in decision-making.

USING OPEN MANAGEMENT

The open system of management, which encourages the exchange of information and views between team members, allows managers and staff to work together creatively. Problems can be discussed and decisions reached quickly and easily. To achieve this, try to make your office open-plan – this will facilitate collaboration. You may also wish to leave your office door open whenever you are available to speak to staff; if this is not practical, make appointments with staff and keep them.

26 Keep staff informed wherever possible – uncertainties are very demotivating.

CHOOSING EFFECTIVE METHODS OF COMMUNICATION

METHODS

FACTORS TO CONSIDER

ELECTRONICS
The variety of methods made possible by the computer age, such as e-mail.

- These are highly effective means of quickly reaching those with whom you are communicating.
- Interaction and participation are possible – and often simple – for all involved parties.
- Their ease of use means that they pose a possible risk of communications overload.
- The seemingly endless possible combinations of words, images, and color are very powerful.

MEETINGS
The basic means of direct people management.

- If used properly, meetings can build relationships and mutual trust.
- Meetings enable instant feedback.
- Meetings facilitate mutual understanding.
- Responses can often be gauged through eye contact.
- Preparation, planning, and openness are required.

JOURNALISM
Takes many forms, from newsletters to full magazines.

- In-house publications enable a wide range of messages and editorial techniques.
- It is possible to facilitate some interaction through readers' letters and contributions.
- The content of most organizations' journals tends to be bland, resulting in low readership.

INTERNAL MARKETING
Consumer techniques applied internally.

- This is a powerful method of "selling" change to the organization's own staff.
- Detailed written documents and colorful posters help explain and simplify complex messages.
- These techniques are able to elicit very strong, immediate motivational responses.

BULLETIN BOARDS
The easiest way of messaging in an organization.

- Bulletin boards can be either official information givers or for general use by employees.
- Bulletin boards provide a central location on which to make information accessible to all employees.
- There is no real possibility of interactive response, and employees may feel uninvolved.

TELEPHONE
A critical tool for one-to-one communication.

- The telephone is not suitable for lengthy or complicated discussions.
- The lack of physical presence may lessen the speakers' understanding of each other.

PROMOTING DISCUSSION

Motivational management encourages and guides discussion about further involvement and contribution. Even issues that are dealt with by formal channels have probably been discussed informally. To this end, it is just as important to have informal talks with your staff as formal team meetings. Invite discussion by posing questions and seeking opinions. Treat contrary views with respect, and when you disagree, explain why fully.

27 Encourage disagreement – it often paves the way to consensus.

MAKING TIME AVAILABLE

Communicating and thinking are important activities in motivational management. Try to avoid becoming so preoccupied with your workload that you run out of time for these activities. Keep a diary in which you analyze your workweek. Eliminate or shorten activities where possible, in order to leave more time for communication and thought. Set aside time for at least one face-to-face discussion or coaching session each week. Remember that to motivate your staff fully it is important to be visible, approachable, and unhurried at all times.

28 Make time to stop and chat rather than simply greeting staff.

Staff member is given opportunity to speak freely

Manager listens to what is being said and offers advice as necessary

◀ **TALKING FACE TO FACE**
You should regularly take the time to talk with each member of your staff. Ask if anything would make his or her job easier, and try your best to fulfill requests.

COMMUNICATING WELL

To motivate team members, engage them in decisions that might affect them, instead of merely informing them after the fact. If people express concern about a new policy, ask how you can allay their concerns. Undertake to report back on any problems that they pinpoint, and let them know how you plan to proceed, using their input. Involving staff from an early stage encourages all members to feel that they can make a difference.

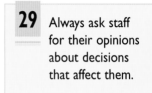

29 Always ask staff for their opinions about decisions that affect them.

POINTS TO REMEMBER

- If the manager does not play favorites, favors are less likely to be sought.
- Honest disagreement can be fruitful, but only if those in dispute share an objective.
- Hidden agendas arouse suspicion.
- False rumors should be quashed as soon as they are heard.
- Ignoring the efforts of "office politicians" often discourages further attempts.

30 Be aware of office politics, and set an example by never taking part yourself.

AVOIDING OFFICE POLITICS

Many work groups are highly political. Members jockey for position, form cliques, spread rumors, curry favors, and backbite. Do not get involved in office politics; indeed, discourage them at every opportunity. Any personal advantage that you may gain will be outweighed by the long-term damage to the organization as energies are diverted away from business. The motivational manager must concentrate on clearly communicated purposes and not allow any deviation from the behavior that promotes those goals.

Manager intervenes to prevent an angry exchange between two staff members

INTERVENING IN ▶ OFFICE POLITICS
If staff become involved in political games, intervene quickly. Make it clear that nobody will win from the exchange, and insist that differences be settled.

CREATING A NO-BLAME CULTURE

A nyone with responsibility – including yourself – must accept their failures. However, to motivate effectively you need a culture in which no blame is laid for failure. Errors should be recognized, then used to improve chances of future success.

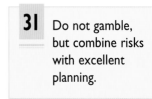

31 Do not gamble, but combine risks with excellent planning.

32 Praise work well done, even if some targets are missed.

33 Take risks only when the chances of success are high.

ACCEPTING RISKS

Management by motivation hinges on delegation and runs two risks: the delegate entrusted with the mission may fail; and the task may fail. To maximize chances of success, you must understand the nature of true risk. This should be a calculated step, not a gamble. Make sure that the delegate is fully briefed before starting the task. Assess the situation, and take action only when the possible and probable outcomes have been systematically weighed and success appears extremely likely. Anything less is generally poor management.

LEARNING FROM MISTAKES

The lessons of failure are valuable, not only to the individuals involved, but also to the organization. Discuss the reasons for failure, so that you can eliminate them and strengthen the platform for success. Taking a constructive and sympathetic attitude to failure will motivate and encourage staff. If you choose to punish failure or motivate by fear, you will not create lasting success. However, make it clear that tolerance of error has its limits. Repetition of the same error is inexcusable, since it shows an inability to learn from mistakes.

QUESTIONS TO ASK YOURSELF

Q What precisely went wrong, when, and where?

Q What were the root causes of the failures?

Q When were the deviations first signaled?

Q Why were the warning signals not acted upon?

Q What could have prevented the failures from occurring?

SOLVING PROBLEMS WITHOUT ATTRIBUTING BLAME

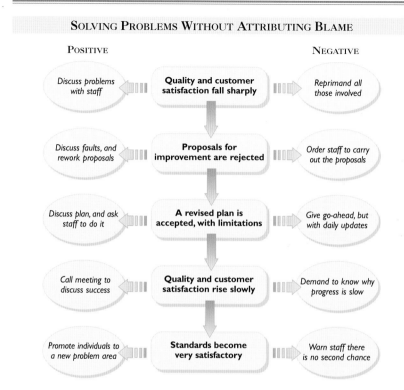

POSITIVE   NEGATIVE

POSITIVE		NEGATIVE
Discuss problems with staff	**Quality and customer satisfaction fall sharply**	Reprimand all those involved
Discuss faults, and rework proposals	**Proposals for improvement are rejected**	Order staff to carry out the proposals
Discuss plan, and ask staff to do it	**A revised plan is accepted, with limitations**	Give go-ahead, but with daily updates
Call meeting to discuss success	**Quality and customer satisfaction rise slowly**	Demand to know why progress is slow
Promote individuals to a new problem area	**Standards become very satisfactory**	Warn staff there is no second chance

USING ACTION REVIEW

Action review is the process of systematically reviewing the success or failure of a project in order to learn from mistakes. The participants in the review agree on the lessons to be learned. They are put on the record and circulated to everyone involved in the project, helping establish what went right and what went wrong, and the reasons why. Use action review to inform staff what they should and should not do in the future and to spotlight the parts of the system that need reform.

34 Be firm but fair when you are drawing attention to error, and do not pull any punches.

WINNING COOPERATION

The basic component of a motivational environment is cooperation, which you must give to your staff, as well as expect from them. It is still essential to be in control and to support your staff while doing so, but be sure not to damage workplace motivation.

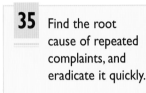

35 Find the root cause of repeated complaints, and eradicate it quickly.

HELPING STAFF

Two key motivational questions to ask your staff are: "What do I do that stops you from doing a better job?" and "What should I do to help you perform better?" If you cooperate by acting on the answers – for example, by investing in new tools or training if requested – you can bring about major improvements in motivation. Not acting on such feedback will demotivate. The prime objective is to help staff to help themselves.

DO'S AND DON'TS

✔ Do follow up on suggestions, requests, and comments made by others.

✔ Do get feedback to ensure that what you say has been fully understood.

✔ Do ask a critic to judge your voice and body language and their impact on audiences.

✔ Do remember that the best discipline is self-discipline.

✗ Don't ask for advice unless you respect the potential adviser.

✗ Don't neglect to provide the right resources if you want the right results.

✗ Don't try to do somebody else's job – even if you are better at it.

✗ Don't leave people without clear instructions and guidelines to follow.

MOVING CONTROL LEVELS

Levels of control vary from an insistence on checking and approving every action, to laissez-faire, in which people are free to perform as they wish and be judged only by the results. Increase motivation by moving toward less rather than more control. To do this, discuss and agree on tasks, objectives, and methods; then allow the implementation to proceed independently, subject only to reports on progress and major deviations. In case of problems, do not rebuke, but consider potential remedies.

36 Always check that your wishes have been understood.

37 Inform staff of the use of their ideas – and success rates.

BEING GENUINE

Feigning a cheerful manner to help you win cooperation can backfire. For example, you may feel that you are successfully hiding the fact that you are tense, but those around you can tell – by your body language and voice tones – that you are faking. A forced smile is often easily recognizable. Try to be open in your appearance and behavior.

38 Have a good reason and an explanation for refusing a request.

Open stance

Welcoming, friendly expression

Tense expression

Hunched shoulders and crossed arms

▲ **HOW YOU SEE YOURSELF**
It is quite possible that you think of yourself as a relaxed, friendly manager, who always welcomes your staff with a smile on your face.

▲ **HOW OTHERS SEE YOU**
Your inner view can differ greatly from external perceptions. Your staff may read your expression as grim and think of you as a grumpy person.

USING VOICE TONE

Always match your tone of voice to the message you are delivering. A genuine smile is audible in the voice, and staff will be more willing to cooperate with a friendly manager. Do not drop your voice at the end of a sentence: it can be dispiriting. Try not to sound worried, or everyone listening will worry. Before an encounter, ask another person to listen as you rehearse and give you advice, if necessary, on how to sound positive.

39 Never offer to finance anything unless you can raise the funds.

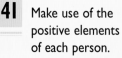

40 Consider ideas from staff at all levels of seniority.

41 Make use of the positive elements of each person.

Supporting Your Staff

If your staff believe that you are standing in their career path, they will rapidly become demotivated. Part of your job is to foster their careers, so you must repress the urge to keep very good people for yourself. Support and encourage your staff, and make the case for them to your seniors if necessary. Remember, though, not to agree to anything that you cannot deliver, and never make promises and then renege. Actions such as these can undermine your authority and inflict a level of motivational damage that cannot be recouped.

Taking an Overview

When analyzing staff motivation, stand back and look at the overall situation. Do not concentrate solely on one set of needs – whether they are team, individual, or task needs. Think about atmosphere, team complaints, and results achieved. Above all, ask lots of questions – you will then form a picture of how the system operates and how well it works.

Task Needs
Determine the task objectives, and consider the problems involved.

Team Needs
Encourage team members to share ideas and to support one another.

Individual Needs
Monitor working conditions, and help staff develop their full potential.

▲ JUGGLING NEEDS
As a manager, there are three "needs" that you must juggle constantly and ensure are equally met: those of the task at hand, of the team, and of the individuals. The needs always overlap and, at times, may conflict.

USING FREE INCENTIVES TO WIN COOPERATION

Free or easy-to-supply incentives are a simple and essential way to win and maintain cooperation. Start by thanking people for a job well done, and follow this up with a written acknowledgment. This is hard for many managers, but is an essential counterweight to criticism. Other ways to increase cooperation include acknowledging staff achievements publicly and holding specific meetings for the purpose of boosting morale. Be friendly and polite at all times – bad manners demotivate – and deal sympathetically with personal requests, such as time off for a special purpose. Play the helpful friend, not demanding employer, in these circumstances.

▲ **PUBLIC RECOGNITION**
If you are with senior managers or clients and notice a member of your team, introduce her to those with you and, if possible, mention her achievements. This type of gesture makes people feel valued.

Manager uses visual aids to show progress achieved

WRITTEN ▶
PRAISE
Always follow up a verbal thank you with a written note. This will emphasize your appreciation while increasing motivation and cooperation levels. Handwritten notes tend to be the most effective.

▲ **MORALE-BOOSTING MEETINGS**
Try to hold regular morale-boosting meetings, especially if your work is full of deadlines and stress. The meetings support staff and help put everyone's minds at ease.

ENCOURAGING INITIATIVE

A sure sign of high motivation is a lot of initiative. The ability to take the initiative depends on empowerment and an environment that recognizes contribution. The more you expect of people, the more they will give, as long as you support them.

42 Give people the opportunity to use their own initiative whenever possible.

ASKING FOR SUGGESTIONS

The results from one survey showed that in the typical company only 4 percent of the ideas for improvement ever reach the top. Do not let that happen. Invite suggestions via a suggestion box, or hold brainstorming meetings. Respond positively to all volunteered ideas. Use marketing devices such as "Idea of the Month" to recognize and encourage good contributions. If at all possible, accept each suggestion, even if it must be modified. If you must reject any ideas, explain to the staff why – and do it with sincere regret.

43 Acknowledge all suggestion box ideas immediately – handle any rejections tactfully.

USING INDIVIDUAL EFFICIENCY PROJECTS

When you find a suggestion that you want to implement, allow the person from whom it came to see it through to fruition. The idea behind this action is that the staff member whose suggestion it was is likely to have the most enthusiasm for it and be very motivated to ensure that it is a success. He or she should be free to delegate the whole task or any of its parts, but it remains that person's responsibility. Use this as one of your chief motivating factors when requesting ideas from your staff, and you are likely to be encouraged by the increased enthusiasm that will result.

▲ WORKING ALONE
If a staff member is eager to take his ideas further, allow the time and allocate the resources to do so.

SETTING HIGH TARGETS

If you think small, that is how you are likely to end up. Set high expectations, and you will find that people rise to the challenge. If you let present performance become your benchmark, your team may never achieve its full potential. However, high expectations must be realistic or demoralization will result. Encourage continual improvement, until it becomes second nature to the organization.

44 Encourage staff to achieve by setting high but realistic targets.

CASE STUDY

A high-growth company reported the first losses in its history, so a new chief executive, Sue Wilde, was promoted from within the organization.
　　Sue was set the seemingly impossible target of making the company the largest in the business within a four-year period. This meant tripling market share against powerful competition. She considered that a massive communication program was a vital requirement. At one mass meeting, Sue asked the staff for suggestions for substantially reducing production costs and underpricing outside suppliers. Having considered all their ideas, Sue allowed her staff to put the most promising ones into practice. As a result, the company went on to reach its market-leading target two years ahead of schedule.

◀ ACHIEVING THE IMPOSSIBLE
Sometimes it is possible to achieve what may seem, at first glance, to be impossible. In this example, the new chief executive successfully motivated the organization's workforce, who took a challenge to its heart and turned around an entire market. It is quite possible that without the extra efforts the organization would have collapsed, with disastrous results for all.

45 Do not be too fast in accepting "No" for an answer.

46 Give your staff a say in the setting of targets.

REVIEWING SYSTEMS

Once you have encouraged initiative and set targets, performance should improve. If there is no discernible improvement, look more closely at the present system, since it may be blocking progress. If so, sweep it away, start afresh, and set new, higher benchmarks. Ask colleagues with high performance records what systems they suggest, and implement the best practice. Both the investigation and the implementation will score high motivationally. A high target set by the staff themselves is a great incentive.

GETTING THE BEST FROM PEOPLE

People are capable of remarkable achievement, significantly ahead of previous performance, if they are provided with the right environment and given the right motivational leadership.

MOTIVATING INDIVIDUALS

Trying to motivate individuals is always tricky because of the variations between them and the way they interact with your own personality and motivation. Remember at all times to serve your ultimate interest – obtaining the right outcome.

47 Stretch people with goals that push them to perform better.

48 Make the most of new staff by first making them feel welcome.

49 Form your own opinions of your colleagues and staff.

ASSESSING INDIVIDUALS

To motivate well, start by assessing the individuals on your team. Once you have done so, you will have a far better idea of the best ways in which to motivate them to achieve their maximum potential.

Always approach people without preconceptions, and concentrate your attention on performance – not on personality, habits, or physical appearance. Liking people is a valuable quality in a good leader; favoritism is not. It demotivates the unfavored and may make the favorite unpopular within the team. Avoid accepting a third party's judgment of a staff member; make up your own mind.

RECOGNIZING DIFFERENCES

To achieve the best results from each individual, it is important that you recognize his or her specific motives and treat people on their own merits. Differences in behavior may be influenced by age, gender, and position on the career ladder.

Give tasks to the most suitable people. For example, a gregarious person will be best at a task that involves meeting people, while someone with a quiet personality may appreciate being given a task that mainly involves working alone. Do not shy away from giving tasks that may develop skills and increase motivation.

CONSIDERING NEEDS ▷

People at different stages in their careers are motivated by different elements of their work. These examples show some typical motivational factors that may influence two very different individuals.

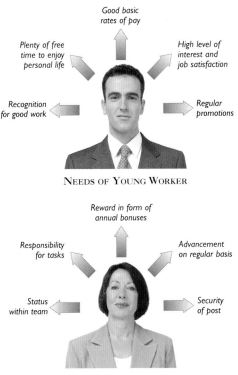

Good basic rates of pay

Plenty of free time to enjoy personal life

High level of interest and job satisfaction

Recognition for good work

Regular promotions

NEEDS OF YOUNG WORKER

Reward in form of annual bonuses

Responsibility for tasks

Advancement on regular basis

Status within team

Security of post

NEEDS OF EXPERIENCED WORKER

50 Be as natural as possible, but tailor your approach to each individual.

TAILORING YOUR ACTIONS

Different people want their managers to play different roles. One may seek a parent figure, while another wants to prove his or her capability. A third may be looking for reassurance. If the role makes sense in management terms, play it. You have to be both soft and hard. Use the appropriate management style for each individual. It is not necessary for everyone on the team to like you, but they must like working for you. Achieve this through firmness as well as friendliness.

OFFERING INCENTIVES

There are many incentives you can offer to help motivate people, and each has different effects. Some of those most commonly used include recognition, money, health and family benefits, and insurance. There tends, however, to be a dividing line between financial and nonfinancial incentives. If you are not in a position to offer financial incentives like pay raises and bonuses, it is still possible to motivate staff by ensuring that the non-financial incentives you offer are attractive to the potential recipient. For example, you might allocate a parking space to someone who drives to work. Think about the general and specific requirements of your staff.

51 Remember that what you measure and reward is what you get.

TAKING A BREAK ▶
Travel incentives – overseas trips, discounts on flights, or just a weekend break, especially when there is no work involved – are all highly motivational. Additionally, the staff member returns to work refreshed.

CASE STUDY
Mary, a departmental manager, had interviewed two internal candidates for a vacancy and had to decide between them. She considered both to be capable but, after much deliberation, felt that Sarah had the edge over Bill.
  Instead of just appointing Sarah and letting Bill hear the news from other sources, Mary arranged a meeting with Bill before announcing Sarah's appointment. Mary felt that

a written memo or an e-mail, however tactfully composed, was the wrong way to inform Bill of her final decision, and would intensify any stress that he was feeling. She explained the reasons behind her decision, emphasizing that Bill was a valued employee, and that the decision had been difficult. Bill appreciated Mary's honesty and accepted her explanation. Because he was treated with respect, he suffered no loss of motivation in his existing job.

◀ **MOTIVATING BY FEEDBACK**
When delivered in the right way, even bad news need not demotivate. In this example, Bill is motivated by the knowledge that Mary thought him to be a valuable staff member. He felt that she was honest with him and that he could still make a positive contribution to the team.

SETTING REALISTIC GOALS

Motivate both teams and individuals by involving them in deciding on budgets, targets, and other goals. Find the right combination of target and reward – one that will maximize effort and achieve economic returns for the company – remembering that no scheme linking rewards to goals can work well unless both aims and thresholds are realistic and fair. For example, if you are trying to reduce costs, advise the team of present cost levels, give them a target figure to work toward, and tell them the figure for the company as a whole. Offer a proportion of their target savings as a reward.

THINGS TO DO

1. Offer a variety of fringe benefits, allowing people to choose from several options.

2. Look for projects in which cash savings can be shared.

3. Use gifts as incentives when cash is not possible.

4. Set realistic timescales if goals are very demanding.

52 Do not put a ceiling on incentives – it limits motivation.

MAKING INCENTIVES WORK

If your staff are earning good salaries and have interesting and responsible jobs and recognition from you as their manager for work well done, they should perform well without constant offers of new incentives. Reserve exceptional incentives for occasions when exceptional effort is required to meet demanding targets. Do not allow staff to expect special rewards for simply doing their jobs.

CHOOSING FROM INCENTIVE OPTIONS

There are many ways in which you can provide incentives to motivate your staff. Try some of the following:

● If you have large enough numbers, group staff into teams and offer a reward to the "winning" team;

● Divide staff into three teams, and split the total reward into first, second, and third "prizes" to reward all the teams;

● Do not set any limits on incentives – devise individual targets for each person;

● Allow people to set their own goals, and link the incentives to ambitions as well as successes;

● Set a threshold – nobody gets anything unless the benchmark is passed;

● Run a lottery in which every 10 percent improvement wins a ticket that enables people to compete for prizes;

● Devise extra incentives for performance early in the financial period in order to get a fast start.

MOTIVATING GROUPS

People behave differently in groups. Mob hysteria is one example. Its benevolent opposite is the spirit of togetherness that can animate groups of any size. Motivate staff by mobilizing support for their group aims and setting strategies for tackling objectives.

53 Ambition dictates achievement, so be sure to encourage big ambitions.

54 Confront trouble-makers as soon as you become aware of their presence.

LEADING A TEAM

Within any group, one person is usually singled out as the team leader. That may be you, but if several teams are working for you, nominate a leader for each. Always be positive with the leaders. Meet regularly with them and the team, and keep motivation levels high by involving everyone in decision-making, praising them for their team's good work, and pointing them in the right direction when things go astray. However, remember that if motivation is poor, it is the leader who is at fault. He or she should be aware of any problems within the group and should be the one responsible for keeping things in check.

CHANGING SYSTEMS

Sometimes, if your system fails, say, the only solution may be to start afresh. It should not be necessary to get rid of a whole team or even any individuals. Indeed, these courses of action may demotivate further. The problem is usually that good people are trapped in a bad system, rather than vice versa. Listen to your staff's problems. Once the initial period of complaint is over and the genuine causes start to surface, they will point the right way to reform. The more the "brave new world" is their own, the better the individuals will feel about – and perform under – the new system.

POINTS TO REMEMBER

- People in groups produce better ideas, since they can bounce ideas off one another.
- Asking staff members to contribute to planning heightens their levels of motivation and feelings of value.
- Staff criticisms should be taken seriously – do not automatically think of critics as troublemakers.
- Meetings, celebrations, and milestones can raise team spirits.

STRETCHING GOALS

A positive state of mind is crucial to reaching goals, so try to instill this in your team. The group that is motivated by a shared vision and that has translated it into practical objectives will notice – and take – more opportunities than one lacking that double focus. Join with others in shaping the vision and the plan. Then encourage and enthuse, so that the reality matches up to the dream. It is important when setting goals not to stop short of the group's capability; indeed, you should go slightly beyond it. For example, a sports coach may set a goal for his or her team to reach the final of a tournament and urge the players to believe in the aim. The danger is that once in the final the group will feel the goal has been reached, whereas they should strive to win that game, too.

55 Cure any bad systems as a first step to conquering poor morale.

56 If demotivation occurs, consider changing your business system.

▼ ACHIEVING "IMPOSSIBLE" GOALS

In order to achieve "impossible" goals, first set yourself or your team a target that you deem to be "perfection"; this is a goal that you will probably never reach. Make this "impossible" goal less daunting by setting another goal: to be halfway to perfection by the end of the first year. This halfway point, once achieved, then becomes the starting point for year two, so set another halfway goal. Motivate staff by celebrating each halfway achievement.

KEY

■ *Current year's progress*

▨ *Previous progress*

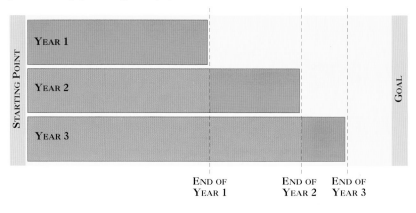

PREVENTING DEMOTIVATION

The course of people management seldom runs smooth, and emotions often run high on both sides of the process. The most valuable technique you can use for preventing demotivation is a sympathetic and understanding human response.

57 Do not wait for annual appraisals to talk about staff performance.

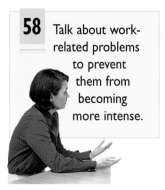

58 Talk about work-related problems to prevent them from becoming more intense.

USING INTERVIEWS

If you find it difficult to motivate staff members, try to establish whether they feel – and are being utilized fully as – part of the team. Arrange interviews with the people involved, leaving them in no doubt about its purpose. Eliminate any fears they may have by striking a positive note at once. Ask them whether they are happy with their working conditions and whether there are any aspects of their jobs they would like to change. Do what you can to improve the situation, and keep any promises you make at the interviews.

TALKING FACE TO FACE

During the interviews, interviewees will hardly ever reply just as expected. However emotional they are, stay calm and collected. Try to establish the reasons for their dissatisfaction as fully as possible. Listen carefully to what they have to say, and try to agree on a resolution. Always be sure to get feedback from interviewees before they leave the room, in order to avoid further misunderstandings by either party. As they depart, remind them that they can come directly to you to talk about any future problems.

59 Allow people to talk about what demotivates them, and listen carefully.

TACKLING PROBLEMS

Personal difficulties and workplace problems are both potential causes of demotivation at work. Never ignore your staff's emotional strains, even if performance is going well, because there is a high probability that the personal troubles will eventually affect work. Your first responsibility must be to the job. At the same time, you must also look after the individual. Approach emotional upsets in the same way as workplace difficulties. First, get the problem clearly defined; then seek the root cause. See if there is a solution that the individual will accept. If so, act upon it. It is important not to let the situation worsen. If you are unable to provide enough help, make sure that you find someone who can.

60 Bad news always travels fast, so deliver it as quickly as possible.

CASE STUDY

A new manager took over the running of a factory and, acting on instructions from above, concluded a long-term contract for the plant's lower-priced output to be supplied by an overseas factory. Rumors about the proposed move had been rife for some time. Once the contract was approved, the manager immediately announced the layoffs that would follow. However, the bad news was coupled with information about an intended major strategic revamp, in order to prevent demotivation caused by the layoffs and the change of management. The manager promised that the new system would increase sales, and announced the introduction of a profit-sharing plan.

Although skeptical, the workforce was motivated enough to give the new system all the effort necessary. As the manager had expected, productivity soared.

DO'S AND DON'TS

✔ Do move away from the desk, which acts as a barrier.

✔ Do show sympathy, however much you feel problems are self-inflicted.

✔ Do make your criticism constructive – you want the person to succeed.

✔ Do keep interviews as short as possible by sticking to the point.

✘ Don't confuse the roles of manager and counselor.

✘ Don't seek to blame individuals for errors.

✘ Don't allow staff members to harbor unfounded fears.

✘ Don't hesitate to discuss difficult personal cases with both colleagues and superiors.

▲ COMMUNICATING TO PREVENT DEMOTIVATION

This case study shows the principles of communicating change and bad news. Deliver bad news quickly, counteracting it with incentives if possible. Tell everyone what is happening, why, and what results you expect, placing emphasis on benefits. This will help prevent demotivation.

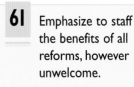

61 Emphasize to staff the benefits of all reforms, however unwelcome.

DEALING WITH DEMOTIVATED PEOPLE

H owever hard you try to prevent staff
   demotivation, you will not always
succeed. Ways of dealing with demotivated
people depend on the situation. A personality
clash between staff members needs different
treatment than demotivation caused by stress.

62 Assess the reasons
for demotivation
before considering
any action.

IDENTIFYING CAUSES

Demotivation must be analyzed before you
can do anything about it. It may be caused by
stress, emotional problems, or physical illness.
Alternatively, there may be something wrong with
the job itself or with the person's approach
to it. Talk to the demotivated person in
order to identify where the problem lies,
and tailor the remedy to the cause – for
example, by getting secretarial help
for someone who is overworked.

▼ SOLVING PROBLEMS
In this example, the manager discovers
that two of his staff members are not
working well together. He steps in to try
to correct the problem. His follow-up
actions determine whether there will
be an improvement in the situation
or complete refusal to collaborate.

Two staff
members are
incompatible
and often
clash at work

Manager
steps in
to calm
situation

ENCOURAGING TEAMWORK

When two members of your staff seem to be constantly at loggerheads, masterly tact is usually required to replace the element of confrontation with collaboration. One course of action is to move the two into a larger team, insisting that they cooperate with and not ignore each other. Another approach is to have the two people swap roles for a while, so that each can gain an understanding of the other's workload. If all else fails, separate the two warring parties permanently to avoid disrupting the work of the entire team.

Manager suggests new ways to work together, and staff members' professional relationship starts to improve

Manager leaves both parties to their own devices, and relationship breaks down

63 Consider all the options before losing valued team members.

COUNSELING STAFF MEMBERS

To cope with the trauma that follows job loss, counseling has become more commonly available in organizations, allowing workers to discuss their reactions to a difficult situation with an impartial, sympathetic listener. You might consider providing counseling as a service even to those whose jobs are secure. They may need to discuss workplace or personal problems that are causing them to feel demotivated. Ideally, a person's counselor will be somebody from outside the company. If there is no option but to use a counselor who is also a staff member, he or she must not have direct or indirect responsibility for the work of the person who is being counseled. Older or more experienced staff members may prefer to talk with a counselor of comparable age and experience.

APPRAISING EFFECTIVELY

O pportunities to motivate your staff will vary according to the current tasks at hand, but appraisals are one way to ensure regular feedback. However, you must remember to follow up properly once the staff appraisals are over.

64 Keep the appraisal relaxed and friendly – do not make it an inquisition.

65 Take the chance to improve yourself by asking staff to appraise you, too.

CONSIDERING AIMS

The true objective of appraisal systems is not to blame, reward, or praise, but to develop. In some progressive organizations, the appraisal is not labeled as such, but is called a "personal development plan" or something similar. Conduct your appraisals properly, and you will help people form an objective view of their past performance. More important, you will also be equipped to encourage better staff performance as well as to enable and assist the interviewee to take on greater responsibility in the future.

STAYING RELAXED ▼

In this appraisal, both manager and interviewee are sitting in a relaxed manner, using reciprocal body language and maintaining strong eye contact.

Staff member holds eye contact, indicating he is relaxed in his manager's company

Manager sits next to staff member to avoid seeming confrontational

DISCUSSING WEAKNESSES

In appraisals, emphasize what the people being appraised have done well – their strengths. You must, of course, also remark on and discuss their weaknesses, but only for improvement's sake. Eliminating weaknesses strengthens performance. However, it is not just staff performance that should be discussed. How does the person being appraised perceive the contribution of the appraiser? Has the manager's conduct throughout the year been helpful and motivating? If not, the appraiser has just as great a responsibility to improve performance as those he or she appraises.

LISTENING TO OPINIONS

Appraisal interviews provide a chance to talk widely over external and internal matters, so do not confine them to issues of personal performance. Remember that all employees are sources of ideas and opinions. Discuss them throughout the year, not just at appraisals. Note the ideas and opinions that you think the organization could benefit from, and consider implementation. The appraisal is ideal for constructive question-and-answer sessions, and you, as the manager and appraiser, should do more listening than talking.

66 Always start appraisals by discussing the progress made and success achieved.

67 Find out about the quality of support given in the job.

ASSESSING MOTIVATION

The appraisal provides a good opportunity to assess staff motivation levels. Be on the lookout for telltale signs of failing interest, such as a lack of enthusiasm for the organization or personal career ambitions. If such signs appear, you must decide how to reverse the process and reinstate a feeling of motivation. You may be able to act before demotivation has a chance to set in fully. Remember that a competent performer will do better at a task that engages his or her full enthusiasm.

FOLLOWING UP
AFTER APPRAISALS

The fact that formal appraisals tend to take place annually does not mean that appraisal is only a once-a-year process. In particular, the formal appraisal contains elements that need to be followed up more regularly – perhaps monthly or quarterly. For instance, if a weakness was diagnosed and training followed, has it been effective? Is the person now confident with that element of his or her job and able to use the new-found knowledge effectively at work? Follow up any interpersonal problems on a quarterly basis. Such follow-up is essential for maintaining the high level of motivation that the appraisal should have triggered. If an appraisal did not motivate, use the follow-up to find out why, and how to get better results.

Review records regularly to make sure improvement is made

Store appraisals in a filing cabinet that you can lock

REFERRING TO RECORDS ▶
Keep appraisal records safely for later reference, in case of any problems. It is also useful to reread the previous appraisal form just before starting on the next one, to see if anything discussed was not implemented.

GIVING FEEDBACK

Appraisal feedback can be positive or negative, one-way or two-way. The result should always be to alter or reinforce behavior. Positive feedback is always welcome, but never give negative personal feedback in public – that is bound to have a demotivating effect. Nor should negative feedback ever be abusive. Focus on one issue at a time, and be highly specific about the past behavior that has generated the feedback and the new behavior that is now wanted. You should also get feedback on your feedback. Make sure your message has been received and understood, and make a mental note of the type of response it provoked.

68 Provide training in small, regular doses rather than one long course.

69 Follow up on any courses to check their quality and staff responses.

DEVELOPING ABILITY

The concept of critical success factors – the elements that organizations need in order to succeed – applies to people, too. Write a list of the key qualities that are needed for a particular task, and assess how they match the qualities of the jobholder. If you feel there is a mismatch – especially one that is likely to cause demotivation – do not reallocate the task, but take immediate action to develop the missing attributes. Abilities are learned and rarely inborn. In almost every case it is possible to be taught a necessary skill, and where abilities are weak they can nearly always be developed. If you feel certain qualities need to be acquired, be sure to provide the training.

PLANNING A CAREER PATH

The appraisal is only one step in a carefully constructed program of planning an individual's career path. It helps both staff and manager to work out the next move and to ensure that training and development are provided before the move, and not after. Appraisals – and their place in the career-planning process – should never be a waste of time and effort, which are precious in every type of organization. Send staff on any necessary training courses before, or as soon as possible after, appointing them to a new task or position; do not allow them to embark on a job for which they are not properly trained. Discuss and agree on a career plan when you make the appointment, and ask the staff member to sign off what you have agreed. Don't let this be something that is handed down from your superiors to your subordinates via you.

70 Give staff chances to use and increase their expertise.

71 Sit in on training courses to ensure the quality is high.

▼ DEVELOPING STAFF
There is a simple yet powerful three-point system that you can apply when you begin developing your staff. Using the system will enable you to focus skills and keep staff motivated.

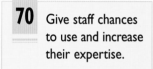

| Evaluate strengths and weaknesses | Ensure job makes full use of strengths | Provide training to improve weaknesses |

EVALUATING EACH JOB

*A*s well as looking at ways to motivate your team as a whole, you need to look at ways to develop individuals and their jobs. Conduct a thorough evaluation of all aspects of each job as well as of the organization's overall system.

> **72** Regard grading and similar systems with caution – not as sacred.

POINTS TO REMEMBER

- The right pay for the right contribution is the perfect pay system.
- If grades are necessary, they should not be encumbered with bureaucratic rules.
- If it is possible, people will turn grades into status symbols.
- Performance must be analyzed from all angles to get a full picture.
- Job specifications should be clearly defined without being overly restrictive.

USING GRADING SYSTEMS

Your organization may run its job and reward system in a rigid, graded way. And you may be in a situation where almost all the factors are outside your control. If that is the case, make the most of the rewards that you are able to distribute. If you are in a position to make such decisions, remember that grading jobs and their holders, and assigning to each grade a salary range, may be useful. However, aim to keep the number of grades as small as possible (in extreme cases, a large organization can have a huge number), the pay ranges as wide as possible, and the importance to staff of the grading system as low as possible.

PUTTING THE JOB FIRST

The key point to remember when evaluating jobs is that the job is more important than the grade, which is merely an administrative convenience. The lure of rising one or two grades may well be motivational, but rules for how many grades staff can advance at any one time, or stating that "a lower grade cannot be the manager of a higher grade," are nonsensical and unnecessary. Get the right person in the right job, and make it clear that the grade goes with the job, not vice versa. If you ask someone about his or her job and the reply is "I'm an 8," take corrective measures.

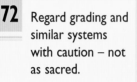

> **73** Pay your staff members for responsibility and contribution, not for seniority and status.

DESIGNING JOBS

Jobs exist to fill roles. If you are in the position of designing a job, your first task is to assign and clarify the job's role and its relationship to the overall task. Be as clear as possible about what the job entails. Every job has its own skills, necessary knowledge, and attributes, so be sure to specify them. There may also be certain legal requirements, terms and conditions of service, and other company stipulations with which the job must comply. Finally, remember that both jobs and their holders need regular modification – and sometimes radical change – over the course of time.

Multiskilling

Variation

Interest

Targets

Prospects

Accountability

Ownership

▲ **ANALYZING JOB CONTENT**
Whatever level of job you are designing, it must be of interest and give satisfaction to the worker. In other words, it must be motivational. Including the factors above will help to make any post more appealing in the long term and motivate the jobholder to perform more effectively.

DEFINING PERFORMANCE

Part of the process of evaluating an existing job – or defining the ideal for a new job – involves looking at past performance levels and deciding what new qualities or tasks are needed to improve them. Arriving at a single measure of performance is difficult. Financial results are the best all-inclusive measure, but do not rely solely on them, since they will convey the wrong message – that only profit counts. They also neglect to show that good short-term results can be gained through bad management, such as cutting back on investment or understaffing. To measure quality, rather than just quantity, include staff morale, customer satisfaction, interteam collaboration, and specific project results as measures of performance.

74 Do not allow job specifications to be perceived as "straitjackets."

75 Ensure that jobs offer a wide range of stimulation and variation.

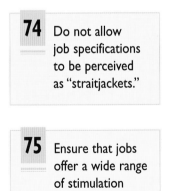

CONSIDERING PAY

When staff members are asked what would raise their motivation, many say, "More money." But money has only a short-term motivational effect. Use pay to reflect good performance, and remember that other motivators may be more effective. The key phrase is "individual circumstances." When you ask a special effort of an individual, however, offering a cash reward in return may work well.

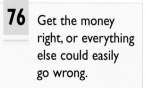

76 Get the money right, or everything else could easily go wrong.

ANALYZING PAY SYSTEMS

REASON FOR PAYMENT	FACTORS TO CONSIDER
TIME Work has been carried out for a specific number of hours.	● It is difficult to monitor the use of working time. ● Payment for fixed hours is not an efficient motivator. ● Effort and hours spent are much less important than individual expertise and quality of contribution.
EXPERTISE Skills possessed by the individual are essential to the job at hand.	● Achievement and recognition are key motivators for staff with expert knowledge. ● Levels of payment are directly related to the amount of demand for specific skills.
INPUT Individual has made a significant contribution to the project, unit, or organization.	● Staff who produce good work should be highly valued. ● It can be difficult to measure an individual's input. ● A good organization encourages innovation, does not penalize mistakes, and rewards creativity imaginatively.
QUALITY OF OUTPUT Work has been of a consistently high standard, enhancing quality of the final product.	● Quality of output is more important than quantity. ● Payments made on this basis result in increased competitiveness among team members. ● Achieving quality standards is motivational.
ACHIEVEMENT Objectives have been met to the satisfaction of those who commissioned the task.	● Rewards offered to project leaders are often linked to the success of the project. ● As workloads are increasingly divided into tasks, more pay is becoming achievement-based.

CONSIDERING PAY PACKAGES

Basic salary raises can dominate pay negotiations. However, wise employers (and wise employees) look at the value of the total package when recruiting and promoting. The other elements, in addition to the basic salary, can be decisive. Profit-sharing and pension plans are very attractive, and non-financial benefits can also be valuable. Be sure that the package you offer compares well with industry and other norms. A competitive pay package can be a highly effective motivating tool.

Salary

Flextime

Paid vacations

Shares

Car

Pension

Insurance

Health care

▲ ANALYZING PACKAGES

A pay package is not just about salary, though that is how most people tend to think of it. Other elements come into play, not all of them directly cash related. Check out packages offered by rival companies, and make sure what you have to offer is comparable.

77 Watch costs of fringe benefits – unwatched, they tend to soar.

78 If you are the highest payer, be sure to get the highest results.

AVOIDING SECRECY

Secrecy is one factor that makes pay a managerial minefield. Usually, people do not know what other people in a unit – or an organization – earn. They tend to make wrong guesses, or else they find out and then feel aggrieved by what they discover. Openness is a great way to promote a sense of fairness. People can accept the principle of unequal pay for unequal achievement, but only in an atmosphere of consensus and cohesion. Encourage both by ensuring that pay levels are discussed openly and with full information. The feelings involved can be painful and deep, though, so treat perceptions of unfairness accordingly. Be sympathetic with people who feel unfairly paid, even when nothing can or should be done.

ENRICHING JOBS

One way to improve motivation is to enrich jobs. The "scientific" management school divided work into component parts, at which each worker, by repetition, became proficient – and bored. Aim for variety, multiskilling, and high interest levels.

79 Delegate whole tasks to improve efficiency and motivation.

RAISING INTEREST LEVELS

The interest in a job depends on the content of the work, its complexity, and the sense of achievement generated by successful completion. You will not raise an assembly line worker's interest, for example, by adding one more repetitive task. Instead, put staff in a manufacturing cell with six people, say, each with interchangeable skills, and make that group responsible for an entire subassembly. That will raise interest levels in the same way as giving a wine-shop assistant expertise in the wines carried. Ideally, give difficult, yet doable jobs to somebody whose personal drive will be engaged by the task.

80 Give staff every opportunity to use newly acquired skills once training has finished.

DEVELOPING SKILLS

The more varied the job content, the greater the need for new skills. Try to apply multidisciplinary, cross-functional working in teams. This helps develop new skills, which may require formal training. Although training may take staff members away from their workloads, it is beneficial in adding to variety and is essentially motivational. Encourage everybody to think of portable skills as their personal capital. Consider making the acquisition of new skills an element in bonuses and pay raises. With good management, the acquired skills of each staff member will more than justify the extra rewards.

POINTS TO REMEMBER

- Real job enrichment produces cost savings as well as increasing motivation.
- Training is both a means to and a form of job enrichment.
- Staff members prefer a difficult job to a boring one.
- Employees like to be considered as experts in their jobs and to be treated accordingly.
- People who have kept valuable suggestions quiet for years should be helped to "open up."

Manager splits a three-part task among three staff members – one task each

Team member is bored with her single task

TEAM

MANAGER

Staff member is happier having three varied tasks

STAFF MEMBER

Manager gives the whole task to one staff member to provide variety

PROVIDING VARIETY

If you give a whole task to one person, instead of splitting it among several, it will add more variety and responsibility to the job. It is also a good way to increase staff involvement and commitment levels as well as develop otherwise unused skills. Provide variety by giving people new tasks, making them members of quality-control and other project teams, sending them on customer visits, and so on. The guiding principle is to stimulate enthusiasm.

▲ EXTENDING SKILLS
When delegating work that is divided into two or more parts, try to give the whole task to one person, providing training where necessary. This saves time on handovers, relieves monotony, and raises motivation for the staff member.

81 When an idea is accepted, let its creator implement the suggestion.

ASKING FOR SUGGESTIONS

Encouraging people to use their initiative to improve efficiency enriches jobs and increases variety. Ask staff for suggestions, and, if possible, act on the answers you receive. Feeling comfortable making suggestions is enriching in itself. Constantly looking to see how a task can be improved adds to the variety. Beware, though, that an atmosphere that has been unresponsive in the past may inhibit people from volunteering ideas.

EMPOWERING STAFF

Most organizations run on rulings that are passed down to the staff from top management; this is demotivating. In contrast, delegating powers traditionally kept at the top not only motivates, but also raises everyone's levels of performance.

82 Make sure that your staff do not suffer under outside limitations.

83 Find out about a job from the person doing it.

USING TEAM MEETINGS ▼
People who want to do a job well are most likely to offer the best advice on improving the system in which they work. Ask your staff to discuss their opinions with you, and listen to what they have to say.

ENCOURAGING INPUT

In most cases, people are experts in their jobs, having improved their skills over time, and they are perfectly capable of both suggesting improvements and implementing those changes. Use these people when seeking improvement. If their knowledge is ignored, staff become demotivated by the neglect and resistant to change imposed from outside. Consult with those affected before making changes, and encourage them to take full responsibility for redesigning their jobs.

Staff member offers advice to senior manager

Senior manager makes full notes of proposed changes

DELEGATING AUTHORITY

Being managed is not in itself a motivating experience. If you are a wise, stimulating manager, those who work for you will be well motivated. However, the more authority is retained at the top, the lower motivation will be. Staff become used to depending on their manager's decisions and authorization, blunting their own initiative and making them dependent. Exercise authority, but not unnecessary force, to achieve desired results. Sharing authority helps develop people's own talents. Delegate downward any tasks that you do not have to do yourself. Look also for whole areas of authority that can be delegated, but always retain overall control.

▼ RAISING ISSUES

Encourage your team to come to you with changes they would like to make to work procedures; discuss their proposals with your superior if necessary. This system is known as "bottom-up" management.

Key

⟶ *Team suggests to manager a change in work procedures*

⟵ *Senior manager, via manager, allows team to try new system*

⟶ *Team reports results to manager, who discusses them with senior*

⟵ *Senior approves new system to be implemented permanently*

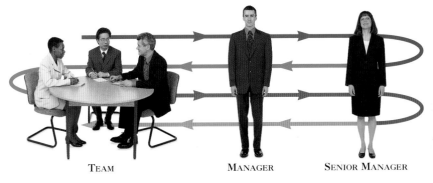

| TEAM | MANAGER | SENIOR MANAGER |

USING UPWARD APPRAISAL

Appraisal of superiors by their subordinates has achieved wide publicity. It has been installed in many organizations, either by itself or as part of a system in which everyone appraises one another. Do not regard this type of appraisal as a cure-all; use it instead to draw attention to areas of potential improvement and to give a different perspective to the manager-staff relationship. Do not allow the process to be used to settle old scores, or people may find it too embarrassing to use properly. A constructive working environment should support and exploit upward appraisal.

BUILDING CAREERS

The ideal career path is smooth and clear of obstacles. Such a path can be highly motivating: encourage your staff to follow it by offering them the support they need to develop the abilities that will ultimately take them on and up.

84 Find an assignment for anyone who has not had one in the past year.

85 Encourage your staff to enroll for regular training – it will pave the way to future success.

USING ASSIGNMENTS

One of the best ways of helping staff in their career progress is by issuing short-term "assignments," which give people the chance to show both their mettle and their ability. Opportunities of this kind are fewer under the old-style, hierarchical methods of career development in which people stay in one job for a set length of time before moving up the ladder. Look out for any chance to broaden staff confidence and experience by giving people tasks, either singly or in a group, that lie outside their normal work. Take an interest in their progress, and debrief often. While your staff are learning, you learn what they can do.

CASE STUDY
Andrea Morgan, a clever and hard-working manager, was swiftly promoted as her abilities grew, but soon her work began to fall below acceptable standards. She had personal difficulties to cope with at home, but this did not fully explain the decline in her performance. A new senior manager made it clear that Andrea had a choice: either improve performance or leave the organization.

In an interview between the two of them, it emerged that Andrea felt frustrated by the underuse of some of her abilities and also by poor leadership from the head of her department.
After some consideration, her senior manager promoted Andrea to that post, in which she succeeded admirably. She paid special attention to – and utilized fully – the abilities of every member of her workforce.

◀ MOVING CAREER-PATH OBSTACLES
There are many reasons why a person's performance might suffer, so do not pass judgment until you have taken the time to talk through any problems. You may find, as in this case, that the career path is being blocked by what the person sees as an immovable obstacle. Find out what it is and move it, or you risk losing valuable staff members.

WIDENING PERSPECTIVES

Most people – possibly unconsciously – undergo a process of self-actualization, moving by trial and error toward the field that suits them best and in which they can achieve to the utmost of their ability. As they grow out of one "phase," they move on. Most people start out with a narrow range of skills and interests; as that broadens, so will their career path. Perspectives will shift, too, from short term to long. As confidence increases, so will self-control and self-awareness. Watch for these signs, and accentuate the positive through regular communication. Be sure that personal goals and the job remain in step, or the person will lose motivation and you will probably lose the person.

86 Do not underuse people – it causes them as much stress as overuse.

87 Utilize as many of each person's skills as possible.

GETTING THE MOST FROM TRAINING

Training can be an end in itself. Learning to learn develops the mind and objectivity. It is useful, as well, in terms of personal development, offering a sense of growth. However, the day-to-day work of an organization also provides plenty of practical reasons for training people. For example, if your company is moving from selling commodities to marketing consumer goods, try to ensure that you and your staff are fully trained in modern marketing techniques. Make sure that skills acquired in training can be used directly in the job. This will overcome the familiar "reentry" problem of the trained individual, bursting with newly acquired knowledge, who meets resistance when trying to implement the new-found information, gets frustrated, and gives up. This is most demotivating.

▲ LEARNING SKILLS
No matter what the job or situation, it is imperative that an individual is taught the necessary skills before you encourage the next career move. For example, a staff member who has the opportunity to work abroad may need to be sent on a language course.

REWARDING ACHIEVEMENT

For rewards to motivate, make sure you encourage competition among staff by acknowledging individual achievement and giving appropriate recognition to highfliers.

RECOGNIZING EXCELLENCE

In the achievement-led style of modern business, outstanding contributions from individuals further careers and earn rewards. Any rewards, however, must be motivational. Reward appropriately any contributions that are of genuine benefit to the organization.

> **88** Seek early chances to promote able, younger members of your staff.

> **89** Use monetary rewards as flexibly as possible to get the most of their motivational value.

EMPHASIZING ACHIEVEMENT

The Japanese have one of the most hierarchical societies, and respect for one's elders is built into their culture. However, age does not come before ability in their organizations. Seniors earn respect, but the best-qualified person gets the job, irrespective of age. The system in the West, too, is becoming less age-led. For example, a project could be given to a young manager to command without upsetting the hierarchy or anyone within it. To make sure talent is allowed to develop, some seniors may have to be moved "sideways" to make room for more able juniors on their way up.

BREAKING WITH TRADITION

The traditional, hierarchical system was ideal for maintaining order within large organizations. Command and feedback flowed through the same channels, via each member of the hierarchy. It was an orderly method for an orderly world, but this system is no longer appropriate. Today, quick completion of tasks is more important than obedience to rules, and high achievers may earn more than their nominal superiors. Encourage staff to accept the new approach, but introduce it gradually to those who are used to the old way.

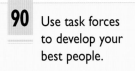

90 Use task forces to develop your best people.

▼ COMPARING ATTITUDES

One of the main differences between people who take a traditional attitude to work and those with a more modern outlook is the length of time that they expect to stay with a company. Traditionalists are more likely to feel that a job is for life.

TRADITIONAL ATTITUDE

MODERN ATTITUDE

Thinks maturity equals seniority

Feels achievement leads to seniority

Expects to receive a good pension

Expects to be headhunted regularly

Feels an allegiance to the organization

Puts own interests equal to the company's

USING A TASK FORCE

A task force is a high-performance, high-morale team set up to undertake a clearly defined task. It fosters leadership qualities and places paramount importance on achievement. Its criteria include:

● A task that is demanding in both time and standards of achievement;
● A single leader, whose role is defined in terms of the task;

● A full-time "core" of staff, who must be completely dedicated. They will be aided as necessary by part-time and temporary team members;
● A special privilege for the leader, who reports directly to top management, bypassing the usual hierarchy;
● Disbandment after the completion of its mission.

MOTIVATING THROUGH CHANGE

Change is a good way to raise levels of achievement, and few things increase staff morale more than successful change. There are two ways to improve – gradually and radically. You must decide which system is best for you in each situation.

91 Take every chance to preach quality and practice improvement.

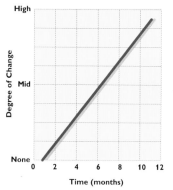

High

Degree of Change

Mid

None

0   2   4   6   8   10   12

Time (months)

▲ **USING KAIZEN**

When using kaizen, set out your planned improvements in the form of a chart showing projected changes over a period of 12 months. Aim for a constant degree of gradual change.

MOTIVATING ▶ THROUGH KAIZEN

The motivational effect of kaizen, applied to an organization that was underperforming, was such that staff redoubled their efforts.

CHANGING GRADUALLY

The concept of continual, gradual change (known as *kaizen*, from the Japanese) has become attractive to Westerners and essential to those who adopt Total Quality Management (TQM), which is about constantly improving every process and product by progressive methods. *Kaizen*, however, is more a way of life in which all staff members are urged to look constantly for ways to improve any element of their performance and to believe that nothing is the best it can be.

CASE STUDY

An organization whose products had acquired a bad reputation in the marketplace decided to adopt *kaizen* as its "religion." Staff members received full training in the techniques of continual improvement and were given specific, measured targets to meet. In addition, they were told that if they felt any elements in their working environment would benefit from change, they should propose a new option. The motivational effect of this was striking, since everyone felt in control of his or her own situation. As soon as one target was met, another higher one was put in its place. Quality improved by leaps and bounds, and the company moved from threatened failure to large profits and a rapidly growing market share.

CHANGING RADICALLY

Another method of change is *kaikaku* (Japanese for "radical change"). *Kaikaku* redefines an organization's entire business, looking at its ultimate purpose and examining every process to see what each contributes to the final goal. It also takes into account how that contribution can be radically improved or, in cases where the process serves no purpose, eliminated.

The problem with *kaizen*, and the reason why many Western companies gave up early with their TQM programs, is that major breakthroughs in one part – or even in several parts – of the system may not add up to a sizable achievement for the organization as a whole. *Kaikaku* forces you to concentrate on only those activities that add value. Having tracked down these activities, you then fix targets far in excess of current levels of achievement. The motivational impact of *kaikaku* is enormous, but staff may be slow to accept its necessity.

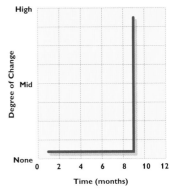

▲ USING KAIKAKU

The projected level of change for an organization using kaikaku *is a period of stability followed by an immediate acute change of direction. As long as staff are properly briefed and each member knows what level of change to expect and what the goal is, it is a highly effective way to implement change – especially in a crisis.*

---

92 Make one major change, while also going for many small ones.

93 Ensure that all staff members are involved in quality-improving schemes.

COMBINING TECHNIQUES

The techniques of *kaizen* and *kaikaku* are not mutually exclusive. The former is a way of life, "the way we do things round here." Everybody accepts the principle that every operation and product or service can always be improved, and that an increase in efficiency will generally result in a rise in profit. The principle of *kaizen* is still applied when an organization is going through radical change. To get the full benefit of *kaikaku*, you will also have to use *kaizen* techniques in the initial revamping and refocusing of activities. Encourage acceptance of radical change in your staff through strategy meetings. At these meetings, it is important to make it clear that no holds will be barred, and to encourage staff to discuss and offer suggestions on any issues.

REWARDING EXCEPTIONAL PERFORMANCE

Staff members are paid for the work they do, but many employers have incentive schemes for exceptional performance. When considering these as an option, work out what constitutes expected performance, and plan a sliding scale for anything above it.

94 Make sure that the rewards you give are the icing – not the cake.

95 Look first at those rewards that do not cost anything to supply.

96 Make contests for nonfinancial rewards as much fun as possible.

DEFINING EXCEPTIONAL PERFORMANCE

The term "exceptional perfomance" is not a fixed, scientific measure. It varies from task to task, job to job, and organization to organization. As a manager, it is important that you recognize and reward what you consider to be genuinely exceptional. To do this, carefully work out, and fix solidly, the levels at which both financial and nonfinancial rewards are triggered off. Seek to ensure not only that good work gets good rewards, but also that top standards are not so high as to be impossible to achieve. You will find that a certain amount of trial and error is inevitable in this process.

REWARDING ACHIEVEMENT

Most incentive schemes tie rewards to sales or profits, or both. Do not reward for achieving budget. Instead, offer rewards at, say, 10 percent intervals above budgeted levels, and inform staff of this. The extra profit should handsomely cover the cost of the reward. You can choose to reward cost reduction, quality improvement, innovation, or customer satisfaction. Rewards must motivate, so monitor the scheme to be sure that they do.

97 Do not let sliding-scale cash rewards become a source of demotivation.

OFFERING NON-FINANCIAL REWARDS

Achievement is its own reward – but it is never enough. Achievers also want recognition. Even a simple "thank you" is an important, underused reward that costs nothing. Staff also value inclusion in events like seminars to discuss company strategy. Such events fit into development programs that are central to sustaining job satisfaction, increasing responsibility, and enhancing career progress and personal growth. Other non-financial rewards such as gifts and vacations may prove cheaper than cash rewards – and everyone loves to receive presents. However, these provide less motivation than individual recognition and are not substitutes for good, year-round management.

CULTURAL DIFFERENCES

Nothing differs more across industry and commerce than the use of money as reward and motivation. Managers in the US may expect large bonuses and stock options, although in Japan, straight salary is dominant and financial motivators are little used. Europe falls in between: mainland Europe being nearer to the Japanese model and Britain closer to the US.

CONSIDERING NONFINANCIAL REWARDS

REWARD	FACTORS TO CONSIDER
RECOGNITION Handwritten note, engraved trophy	● An often-overlooked form of reward that is personal as well as effective in both the short and the long term.
GIFTS AND PRIVILEGES Vacations, sports events, merchandise	● Immediate, and stimulating in the short term. ● May not meet long-term motivational needs.
SPECIAL EVENTS Weekends away, parties, theater trips	● Involve staff from all levels. ● Can stimulate, relax, bond, and motivate staff.
PROFESSIONAL TRAINING On- or off-site courses	● Effective, focused training brings high returns. ● Company gains a qualified employee, who feels valued.
SELF-DEVELOPMENT Personal, nonvocational training	● Very high motivational value. ● Enhancing self-image raises performance levels at work.
EQUIPMENT Company car, laptop computer	● Expensive equipment is highly motivational. ● Need to ensure that equipment is fully utilized.

Offering Cash Rewards

Use rewards in the form of pay increases or financial benefits to recognize achievement, prevent a high-flying staff member from leaving the organization, or encourage an individual to take a greater level of responsibility in his or her job. Remember, however, that this type of reward often has only short-term motivational value. It can also lead to resentment among other staff members and discourage interaction within a team.

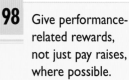

98 Give performance-related rewards, not just pay raises, where possible.

Considering Financial Rewards

Reward	Factors to Consider
Salary Increases Increases in basic rate of pay.	● Money is a powerful short-term motivator: the bigger the raise, the higher the motivation. ● The impact wears off relatively quickly.
Commissions and Bonuses One-time payments linked to targets.	● Increases motivation and job satisfaction. ● There can be difficulties in fixing rates and relating these rewards to base pay.
Performance-Related Pay Regular wage increases based on target-linked performance.	● Is motivational and can be a tax-effective incentive. ● There may be a delay between earning and receiving performance-related pay, thus weakening its impact.
Shares/Stock Options Gifts of shares, or the chance to buy shares at a fraction of actual value.	● Encourages long-term loyalty and sense of involvement. ● A highly effective motivator, as pay-off can be substantial. ● Reward is not immediate, and initial benefit may be small.
Special Rates Help with mortgage/rent, insurance, and other items within tax limits.	● Has considerable staff-retention value and can act as "golden handcuffs." ● Has low motivational value.
Family Health Benefits Paid or subsidized plans offering a wide range of health-care options.	● It is in an organization's interest to have healthy staff. ● Has low motivational value because health-care provision is expected from organizations.

CELEBRATING SUCCESS

Personal thanks for exceptional performance are powerfully reinforced by being repeated or given at a public celebration. Celebrate success, and you can motivate everybody in the unit, not just the achiever. External awards and dinners have proliferated, and few industries are now without them. Pay for entries and tables at these events, and make a fuss of any winners. The same format applied internally is also effective. If a whole team, rather than an individual, is involved, celebration is highly appropriate. Parties give you the chance to motivate by words and by singling out special contributions. Ensure, however, that any event of this type is carefully planned and well staged. Skimping on any elements, especially the catering, is a false economy in terms of motivation.

> **99** Use certificates and engraved presents as reminders of high achievement.

THROWING A PARTY ▶
A staff party is a great way to show your appreciation to all the people who work for you. It is also the ideal setting for rewarding or speaking about exceptional performers.

SETTING PERSONAL TARGETS

Set yourself personal career targets in order to achieve exceptional performance. Ask yourself the following questions:

- What do you want to have achieved in one, three, and five years from now?
- What developments, knowledge, and experience can make your aims possible?
- What can you do to acquire the necessary skills to attain your targets, and how long will it take you to master each of these skills?
- Are there any midway points in your program that will allow you to check progress and make revisions if necessary?

Keeping Motivation High

Once you have successfully raised the motivation levels of your staff, it is important that they stay raised. Varying working conditions, improving management systems, and placing a high value on your employees should all be top priorities.

100 Change your own working methods if it will improve staff motivation.

101 Check on morale levels by talking to staff members on a regular basis.

Monitoring Motivation

People want to feel good about their work and their organization. Encourage and nurture this natural drive – do not spend your time cracking whips and shouting slogans. Use surveys, research, and polling to check on morale and find out when and where new initiatives are needed. Select trusted people to talk to you informally about general mood, developments that affect motivation, and potential problem individuals.

Modifying Practices

In 1927 psychologist Elton Mayo discovered that output increased every time a change was made in working conditions. Also, absenteeism declined during the period of change by 80 percent. The explanation he gave is that people respond to attention. Taking part in experiments and cooperating in changes heightens interest, team spirit, and self-esteem, regardless of the change. Any aspect of motivational practice is open to change. Look for ways to engage all staff in reviewing processes and practices, and in devising ways of changing them. If you find any current practice demotivates, correct it immediately.

Amy is regularly turning up late for work and showing other signs of demotivation – she is asked by her manager to be more prompt

REVIEWING SYSTEMS

Underperformance is expensive, yet 85 percent of all recorded underperformance is thought to result from the system imposed by managers. Do not let that be yours. Review every aspect of your business system regularly. All business systems are capable of demotivating staff, and all are open to improvement. Poor systems generate poor morale. Regularly test your system, and ask for improvement suggestions from those who are on the front line. Remember that the act of reform itself improves morale. Even if your system was motivational when it was originally set up, changing conditions mean that you should always be open to revisions – whether the initiative comes from you or from your staff. Above all, treat seriously all comments on the system – staff will often bring matters to you as a last resort.

THINGS TO DO

1. Look for areas suitable for experimental changes.
2. Use inspiring names for your motivational projects.
3. Keep track of staff morale.
4. Ask staff to inform you of any system problems.
5. Modify or drop any changes that do not work.
6. Give low performers plenty of encouragement.

Amy's timekeeping starts to improve but she continues to underperform – her manager asks her why

A vacancy arises in Amy's new field and she is promoted to it, raising her motivation level further

Amy reveals that poor job prospects are making her feel demotivated – she is sent on a skills-development course

◀ **INVESTING IN STAFF**
This staff member has become demotivated, and her attitude to work has plummeted. Instead of issuing a reprimand, her manager decides to invest in her future career by offering her training with a view to promotion.

ARE YOU A GOOD MOTIVATOR?

Gauge your ability as a motivational manager by responding to the following statements, and mark the options closest to your experience. Be as honest as you can: if your answer is "never," mark Option 1; if it is "always," mark Option 4; and so on. Add your scores together, and refer to the Analysis to see how you scored. Use your answers to identify the areas that need improving.

OPTIONS

1 Never

2 Occasionally

3 Frequently

4 Always

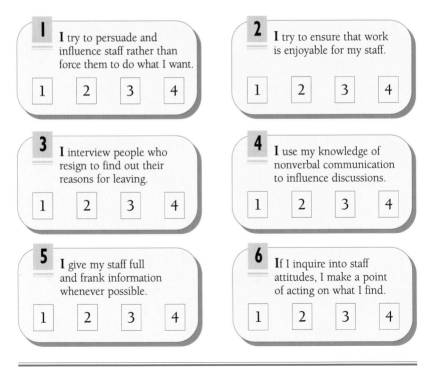

1 I try to persuade and influence staff rather than force them to do what I want.
1 2 3 4

2 I try to ensure that work is enjoyable for my staff.
1 2 3 4

3 I interview people who resign to find out their reasons for leaving.
1 2 3 4

4 I use my knowledge of nonverbal communication to influence discussions.
1 2 3 4

5 I give my staff full and frank information whenever possible.
1 2 3 4

6 If I inquire into staff attitudes, I make a point of acting on what I find.
1 2 3 4

7 I apply Theory-Y management principles rather than Theory X.

1   2   3   4

8 I avoid office politics and discourage others from politicking.

1   2   3   4

9 I involve people in issues at the earliest possible opportunity.

1   2   3   4

10 I give reasons for my actions and for any disagreements with people.

1   2   3   4

11 I seek consensus and encourage others to do the same.

1   2   3   4

12 I react to failure not by blame but by analysis and correction.

1   2   3   4

13 I seek a balance between firm control and giving people independence.

1   2   3   4

14 I make conscious efforts to improve my motivational skills.

1   2   3   4

15 I change benchmarks to keep targets at stimulating heights.

1   2   3   4

16 I revise the system in order to remove obstacles to performance.

1   2   3   4

17 I look at more than just financial results when assessing staff performance.

1 2 3 4

18 I encourage people to be open about how much they and others are paid.

1 2 3 4

19 In appraisal interviews, I request and receive appraisals of myself.

1 2 3 4

20 I get full, clear feedback from people whose behavior I have had to criticize.

1 2 3 4

21 I organize work so that one person can complete an entire task.

1 2 3 4

22 I look at assignments and moves as ways to develop people.

1 2 3 4

23 I encourage people to act on their own initiatives.

1 2 3 4

24 I delegate work that does not have to be done by me.

1 2 3 4

25 If difficult "people decisions" are needed, I make them willingly.

1 2 3 4

26 I act to avert or settle disputes and personality clashes.

1 2 3 4

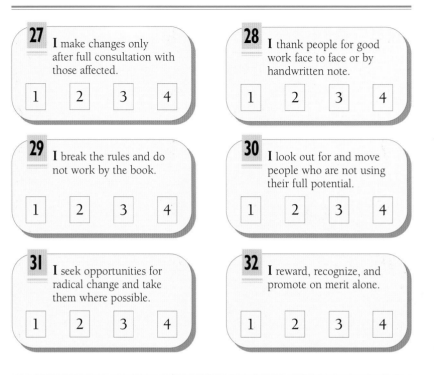

27 I make changes only after full consultation with those affected.

| 1 | 2 | 3 | 4 |

28 I thank people for good work face to face or by handwritten note.

| 1 | 2 | 3 | 4 |

29 I break the rules and do not work by the book.

| 1 | 2 | 3 | 4 |

30 I look out for and move people who are not using their full potential.

| 1 | 2 | 3 | 4 |

31 I seek opportunities for radical change and take them where possible.

| 1 | 2 | 3 | 4 |

32 I reward, recognize, and promote on merit alone.

| 1 | 2 | 3 | 4 |

ANALYSIS

Now you have completed the assessment, add up your total score and check your performance by reading the corresponding evaluation. Identify your weakest areas, and refer to the relevant sections in this book to develop or hone your skills.

32–63: You are probably demotivating rather than motivating your people. You must have noticed that some actions work better than others. Practise them often, and the pay-off will be immediately obvious.

64–95: You know and practise much that is motivationally sound. However, you can reduce your number of missed opportunities by giving motivation your continual attention.

96–128: If you have been honest in your responses to the assessment, you are a motivational marvel! Do not let your high standards slip.

INDEX

ACKNOWLEDGMENT

AUTHOR'S ACKNOWLEDGMENTS

This book owes its existence to the perceptive inspiration of Stephanie Jackson and Nigel Duffie
Dorling Kindersley; and I owe more than I can say to the expertise and enthusiasm of Jane Simm
and all the editorial and design staff who worked on the project. I am also greatly indebted to the
colleagues, friends, and other management luminaries on whose wisdom and information I have d

PUBLISHER'S ACKNOWLEDGMENTS

Dorling Kindersley would like to thank Jayne Jones and Emma Lawson for their valuable par
in the planning and development of this series, everyone who generously lent props for
the photoshoots, and the following for their help and participation:

Editorial Tracey Beresford, Jennifer Boniello, Christopher Gordon, Victoria Wilks;
Design Helen Benfield, Kate Poole; **DTP assistance** Rachel Symons;
Consultants Josephine Bryan, Jane Lyle; **Indexer** Hilary Bird; **Proofreader** Helen Partington
Photography Steve Gorton; **Photographer's assistant** Sarah Ashun;
Photographic coordinator Laura Watson.

Models Philip Argent, Marian Broderick, Angela Cameron, Kuo Kang Chen, Roberto Costa,
Felicity Crowe, Patrick Dobbs, Carole Evans, Vosjava Fahkro, John Gillard, Maggie Mant, Sotiris Me
Ted Nixon, Kiran Shah, Lois Sharland, Wendy Yun; **Make-up** Elizabeth Burrage, Lynne Maning

Special thanks to the following for their help throughout the series:
Ron and Chris at Clark Davis & Co. Ltd for stationery and furniture supplies; Pam Bennett an
the staff at Jones Bootmakers, Covent Garden, for the loan of footwear; Alan Pfaff and the staff
Moss Bros, Covent Garden, for the loan of the men's suits; David Bailey for his help and time
Graham Preston and the staff at Staverton for their time and space.

Suppliers Austin Reed, Church & Co., Compaq, David Clulow Opticians,
Elonex, Escada, Filofax, Gateway 2000, Mucci Bags.

Picture researchers Victoria Peel, Sam Ruston; **Picture librarian** Sue Hadley.

PICTURE CREDITS

Key: *b* bottom, *c* center, *l* left, *r* right, *t* top
Ace Photo Library: Zephyr Pictures 4–5; **Pictor International, London** 34*cr*, 47*tr*, 49*tr*;
Tony Stone Images: Bruce Ayres 6*bl*, 63*cr*; Christopher Bissel 9*br*; Loren Santow 55*br.*
Front cover **Ace Photo Library**: Zephyr Pictures *cl.*

AUTHOR'S BIOGRAPHY

Robert Heller is a leading authority in the world of management consulting and was the founding
of Britain's top management magazine, *Management Today*. He is much in demand as a conference sp
Europe, North and South America, and the Far East. As editorial director of Haymarket Publishing
Robert Heller supervised the launch of several highly successful magazines such as *Campaign*, *Com*
and *Accountancy Age*. His many acclaimed – and worldwide best-selling – books include *The Naked N*
Culture Shock, *The Age of the Common Millionaire*, *The Way to Win* (with Will Carling), *The Complete*
to Modern Management, and *In Search of European Excellence*.